Dedicated to my students,
- Mrs. Dorcely

This book belongs to:

_____

**This is a police car.
A police car has wheels.**

**This is a fire truck.
A fire truck has wheels.**

**This is a red motorcycle.
A motorcycle has wheels.**

**This is an orange car.
A car has wheels.**

**This is a white truck.
A truck has wheels.**

**This is a yellow school bus.
A school bus has wheels.**

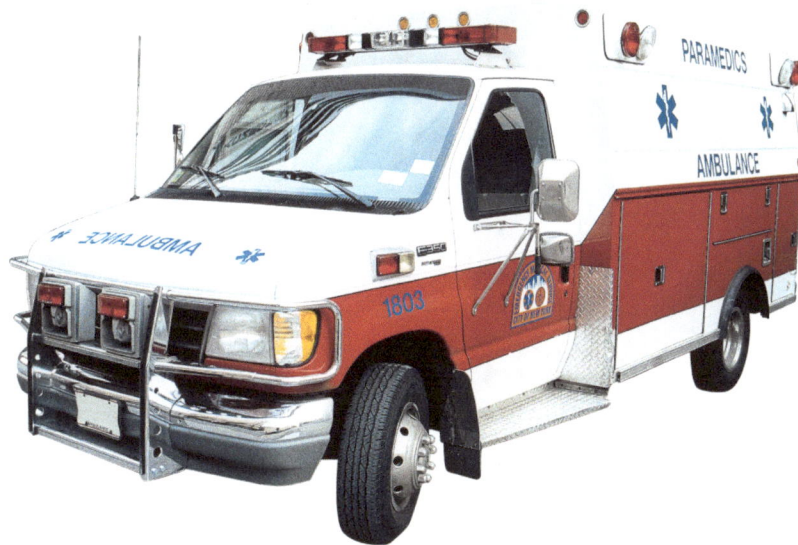

**This is an ambulance.
An ambulance has wheels.**

This is a purple bicycle.
A bicycle has wheels.

**This is a yellow taxi.
A taxi has wheels.**

**This is a pink scooter.
The scooter has wheels.**

**This is a red wagon.
A wagon has wheels.**

**This is a blue wheelbarrow.
A wheelbarrow has wheels.**

**This is a brown train.
A train has wheels.**

**These are gray roller skates.
Roller skates have wheels.**

**This is a green garbage truck.
A garbage truck has wheels.**

**This is a black skateboard.
A skateboard has wheels.**

Your turn!
What else has wheels?

car

garbage truck

wheelbarrow

wheel

wagon

scooter

taxi

bicycle

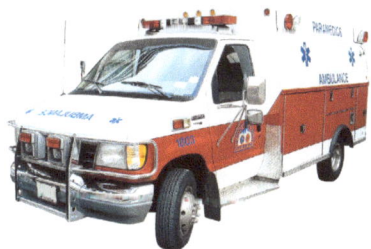

ambulance

Skateboard

school bus

truck

motorcyclet

fire truck

police car

train

roller skates

blue

red

green

orange

white

brown

black

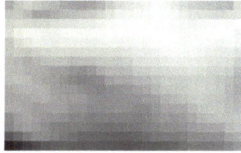

gray

pink

purple

yellow

www.ingramcontent.com/pod-product-compliance
Lightning Source LLC
LaVergne TN
LVHW072102070426
835508LV00002B/228